What Will a Website Do
For Your Business?

Gain Customers

Increase Sales

Brand you as the Expert

By Faye Bond

www.bondglobalenterprises.com

"Where passion, empowerment and business meet"

Copyright Notice

Copyright @ 2011 Bond Global Enterprises, LLC.

All rights reserved worldwide

ISBN: 9781461100171

Preface

Too often you hear of people asking the question – Why Have a Website, they cost too much, then there is all that tech geeky stuff and it wastes a lot of my time?

Yes, websites do cost money to build and they can be too geeky but it is really a waste of your time? Turn it the other way. It would be a waste of your time NOT to have a website.

This 11 point report explains the basic principles of What Will a Website Do For Your Business.

After hours of research and talking with fellow Internet marketers we have all come up with the same conclusion a website is a must for today's businesses.

Connecting your website with social media is a great way to grow your business.

Faye Bond

January 2011
New Zealand

Contents

Introduction

INTRODUCTION

Too often you hear of people asking the question – Why Have a Website, they cost too much, then there is all that tech geeky stuff and it wastes a lot of my time?

The biggest complaint from people is that a website costs too much. In some cases this is true. If you want a custom designed e-commerce, site that has hundreds of pages, products and services and has all the bells and whistles, then it will cost you a fortune.

You could opt to build your own website using free website and hosting services sites. It will cost you nothing but there are serious flaws in these types of websites. Three of these are YOU DO NOT own your domain name, or own content and your site can be taken offline at any time and you would have lost everything. Once down they are gone into cyberspace forever.

If your website is to sell a YOUR products or services then you should choose a website designer that can custom design your site to fit your market, your needs and your price.

What is the most cost effective marketing tool that your business could ever possibly have? It's YOUR WEBSITE. Today business owners are realizing that the best way to find new customers and generate an income is by having an online presence.

It is estimated that approximately 8 million web pages are coming online each and every day. Social media sites like FaceBook and Twitter are booming as more people join up. Business owners are generating more income through their websites.

A website's primary function is to get customers to take the next step or action by either purchasing your product or service, emailing you a question or taking up your offer of a free gift. It is your offline brochure but with a huge difference – your customers and visitors can search your site and dig deeper into the information that you provide.

The opportunity is there for you and your business to find new customers, generate an income and help your customers by sharing your products and services.

Chapter 1

Unlike most brick and mortar businesses, a website is accessible 24 hours a day, 7 days a week, 365 days a year. Your customers can visit your website at any time that is convenient to them. This constant accessibility leads to more business.

Orders can be placed at any time of the day or night. These purchases would have been lost to your competitors.

You are providing your digital services and information around the clock, and with no effort on your part. Delivery of digital media is immediate and captures buyers there and then.

Websites help your customers find you in the offline world as well – your office, your storefront, your phone number and your email address.

Chapter 2

FIND HUNGRY BUYERS

Your website's home page should be designed and written to reach new markets and find hungry buyers for your products and services. To achieve this consideration must be given to SEO or search engine optimization.

SEO focuses on tweaking websites to rank high in search engines like Google and Yahoo. When a user performs a search they use phrases that are called 'keywords'. Using these phrases in the content of your website you will reach new markets and find hungry buyers.

How many times those and other relevant keywords are used on a web page is critical to influencing the ranking that search engine place on the website.

Another SEO tactic is the use of the title and description tags. It is very important to place keywords in title tags. Keep the title tags short and specific as the search engine spiders only read the first 60 – 70 characters.

Search engines place a lot of importance on a site's content when it assesses relevancy to a particular topic. By making keywords in bold and linking to another page search engines can also determine the importance of a word or phrase.

Site structure plays a role in search engine rankings as they aim to find sites that are logically constructed and provide users with simple navigation. Having a sitemap on your site will help search engines to see all your web pages.

Chapter 3

REACH NEW MARKETS WITH A GLOBAL AUDIENCE

Even if your business is run by one person, where the office is a computer and printer tucked away in the corner of your bedroom, once your website is live on the World Wide Web it can be viewed by people from all over the world.

As the world is become more connected and people in more and more countries are becoming active online, your business, no matter how small, will become a global enterprise.

To reach your global audience, make sure your website is global-friendly, which means – It doesn't put up any obstacles to its visitors.

Here are some tips on having a global-friendly website:

- Keep the language simple. Keep words and sentences short. Avoid professional jargon as well as common slang.

- Be consistent in your use of terminology, and have a FAQ page to help your visitors and customers.

- When quoting prices, stated what currency it is in. For example $US100.00.

Chapter 4

SELL AND PROMOTE YOUR PRODUCTS AND SERVICES

Your website is your shop-front. You will not have to pay overheads such as rent, and utilities that a brick-n-mortar business has. Selling on the Internet is a much cheaper way to get your business rolling.

Promoting your products and services can be done easily on the Internet by having search engine optimized pages. There are endless ways to promote your products and services by using free and paid for methods.

Here are a few free ways to promote your website:

Submit your website to search engines – Google, Yahoo, DMoz to name a couple. Writing your site description is important and spending some extra time to write a keyword rich chescription is one step that is highly recommended.

Blog: Post keyword rich articles to your blog and through social media sites such as FaceBook and Twitter.

Article Directories: Write and submit your articles. In your article you add a small bio and links to your website. It is important that you read the rules and regulations of each article directory in relation to how many links you can put in your article. Some article directories are www.ezinearticles.com, www.goarticles.com and www.ehow.com

Signature: In everything you do in relation to your business have your signature on it. This includes emails, articles, posts to your blog, books, videos etc.

Chapter 5

PRESENT A PROFESSIONAL IMAGE

The face of your business is 'A Stage'. You are on show every time someone visits your website. Your professional image is very important as it can affect the number of clients you will be able to attract and keep. Your website is the first contact visitors have when they go online to search for your products and services.

A professional image is a combination of vision, thought, feeling, belief and opinion that others have about you, your company and your products and services. It is not what you think or feel about your company. It's how you are perceived by your visitors in those first few critical seconds that matter.

Professional image design has been described as a simple and complex concept. Your image needs to be something that can easily be described by someone. For example Nike has a check mark or tick as a logo and their tagline is 'Just Do It'. It looks and is simple. It conveys am attitude that makes you want to just do it.

Visitors to your website need to see at a glance that your business name and logo is visually appealing and your slogan is:

- Short and easy to remember. Let it say something about your business but not everything.

- Conveys what is special about you and your business. This distinguishes you from your competitors.

- Says something you want potential customers to remember or feel. When a tagline gives a feeling of empowerment then an emotional bond between you and your customer is formed.

- You use it everywhere. On your website and all your marketing materials.

Chapter 6

IMPROVE CUSTOMER SERVICE

When visitors buy your products and services they are also buying good feelings and solutions to their problems. Most customer needs are based on emotions not logic. They have a problem that they want fixed. Not tomorrow, but now, today!

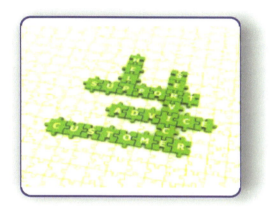

Your customers need to feel important and appreciated. Use their first name and treat them as individuals. This way you will gain their trust and respect.

Help your customers understand your products and services. You may have the best on the market but if your customers don't understand them they will get confused, impatient and angry. Take time to explain how your products and services work. Always look for ways to help your customers. When they have a request, tell them that you can do it. Figure it out afterwards. And always do what you say you are going to do.

When something goes wrong, apologize. Deal with the problems immediately and let your customers know what you have done. People like honesty. Have a simple way for your customers to contact you to complain or compliment. Both complaints and compliments are an opportunity for improvement.

Over-deliver to your customers. This will put your business above your competition. Think of ways you can give more to your customers. Consider giving something for free and follow-up with your non-paying visitors.

Get feedback from your customers and visitors. Ask for suggestions about how you can improve your products and services. Listen carefully to what they say, think and feel about your products and services. Great customer service is all about getting your customers to come back and buy more. It's about giving your customers' good feelings and that you have solved their most pressing problems.

Chapter 7

COST EFFECTIVE MARKETING – SAVING YOU TIME AND MONEY

Marketing your business website should be looked on as an investment. You business will fail unless you get the word out to your customers. There are many resources that you can use to market your products and services. Some of these are:

Social Media Sites – Just watch television or listen to the radio and you will hear something about Twitter or Facebook or Youtube. Many businesses big and small have an online presence on social media sites. Create your profile and start interacting with the community. Include each of your social media links on your website and don't forget to link from your social media site back to your website. The visitors will come.

Write a Newsletter – Newsletters are a great way to communicate with your website visitors. This can be as simple as sending out email updates about new products and services. The tone of your newsletter is like speaking to someone face to face – lively, chatty and yet informative and clear on what you are offering your visitors.

Start a Blog – Probably the best way to start to build a relationship with your website visitors. A blog is an online journal about your business that is regularly updated. Your visitors can interact with you and other visitors by posting comments on your latest journal entry or post as it's called. They can also subscribe to an RSS feed, which will let them know when a new post has been added to your blog. On your blog you should also include your newsletter and your links to your social media sites.

By combining your blog with social media you have the best chance of building solid relationships with your site visitors and will save you time and money.

Chapter 8

COMMUNICATE UP TO DATE INFORMATION TO YOUR VISITORS AND BUILD CREDIBILITY AND TRUST

The Internet is the go-to place for people to find information. It exists in large quantities and is constantly being created and revised. It can be as facts, opinions, stories and statistics and is created for many purposes. Information published on the Internet is designed to inform, persuade and sell.

By giving helpful, consistent, accurate and up to date information to your website visitors and clients you are establishing you and your business as the 'Expert'. The one they can believe and trust to answer their questions and solve their particular problems.

By listening and engaging in conversations with people you are building relationships. They will come to rely on you and use you as a resource. When you go the extra mile by sharing your knowledge to someone they will feel valued and come back for more.

Being accessible and responding promptly to calls and emails will build credibility and trust. Take the time to care about the details as 'It's the little things that matter.'

Chapter 9

KEEP UP WITH THE COMPETITION

One of the secrets to business success is knowing your competition. When you first started your business you would have performed market research on your competitors. That research would have shown you what services and products they were supplying as well as how they were marketing their business. As our businesses grow we tend to get wrapped up in the day to day processes that we forget to keep a finger on the pulse of our competitors.

Here are a couple of ways to monitor and keep you up with the competition:

Google Alerts: For each competitor and specific search term, set up an Alert. Go to http://www.google.com/alerts and enter the search term you want to use, the type of information do you want to receive, how often and how much volume. Enter your email address that you use every day. That way you be continually notified of what they are up to.

Blogs: If your competitors have a blog subscribe to their RSS feed. Each time they put up a new post to their blog you will receive an update.

Social Media: Visit their Facebook page and follow them on Twitter to see what they are doing. Businesses are using social media to inform and listen to their customers. You will gain new insight into what they are planning in the future.

Your competitors are the benchmark for your business. Follow them, learn from, turn their weakness into an opportunity, for success, for your business.

Do it bigger and better!

Chapter 10

COLLATE VALUABLE INFORMATION ABOUT YOUR SUBSCRIBERS

Every business needs to focus on collecting detailed contact information on their subscribers to effectively market your offerings. But, how do you collect this in the first place.

- **Be Open:** Put an e-mail sign up box on the right-hand side (near the top) of your home page. Tell your customers that you would like their name and email address and in return "offer" something that your potential customers will perceive as being valuable to them. The offers could include a subscription to your e-newsletter, weekly or monthly hints and tips or software.

- **Privacy Policy:** Always include a link to your Privacy Policy and tell people clearly what you do with their information. For example "Your information is confidential and will only be used by me'.

- **Delivery:** Tell your subscribers that they will get instant delivery of your valuable offer to their email address.

- **After:** Send emails out to your subscribers asking how you can help them.

Chapter 11

WEBSITES - OVERVIEW

If you want an easy way to manage your small business website, you have a lot of options. There are free resources that you can use to build your own website and some businesses do. I don't recommend these as you do not own your domain name, or your content and your website can be taken down at any time and without reason. You are then left with nothing. And all your hard work has been lost. Gone!

Some free resources do not allow you to have a fully functioning e-commerce site, thus restricting you and your customers in how they purchase your products and services.

There are other resources that you pay exorbitant hosting fees to get your so-called free website. They have templates where you put your site information in and it's done. The down-side to this is that you will have little or no help from anyone.

I often recommend the WordPress platform as a good option because you as the owner can edit the content yourself. You can customize your site using countless standard templates and plugins (enhancement functions). You can use the standard theme or purchase a premium theme that be optimized so that you have all the bells and whistles or you can keep it simple.

As I've introduced small business owners to WordPress and telling them how easy it is to use, I've discovered that they don't necessarily find it to be easy. It offers too many options, too many menus and for those who are technophobic, it's just not for them. And most of all they also tell me that they don't want to spend the time to learn how to set up their website, as it is too frustrating. But wow, once they have their website up and running they are out of the starting gates and ready to have success with their online business.

Chapter 12

WEBSITES

Many small business website owners create their own website and upload it to the Internet and wait for visitors to arrive. In reality the creation and uploading of your website should be the result of your planning. Here are...

1. **What is the purpose and goal of your website?**

   Before you start planning your website you need to define the purpose of your website. Your Business Plan will have defined what products and services you are selling, along with the goals of your business. This way you can easily see where your business is at now and where you see your business being in the future.

2. **Who is my target audience?**

   Researching your target market is often overlooked by businesses but is vitally important and should be one of the main elements for your Business Plan. If you don't know your target audience how will you know what type of website they respond to. For example if your target audience is the elderly, they need a larger typeface and more modern-friendly pages than if you are targeting corporate executives.

3. **How much will I depend on search engine traffic?**

   Search engines like lots of regular and relevant text and videos that are placed on popular sites, e.g. Youtube). By using keyword rich articles and pages you can achieve page 1 on the search engines. When you researched your target audience you would have found many keywords and keyword phrases that are being searched for. Tip: Search for solutions to their problems and pains. Put these keyword phrases as headings in your articles.

4. How much time do I have for updating the website?

Websites that are content related need to be added to and updated to stay fresh for search engine friendliness and to keep your customers happy. Content management systems and tools can make this process easy as your products and articles can be added to a database and with one click you upload it to the Internet.

5. How are visitors going to contact me?

To show that you are a credible business your email addresses should be attached to your domain name, e.g. info [at] yourdomain [dot] com. The use of free email accounts does not portray professionalism and should not be used. The physical address and phone numbers of your business should be on your website. A good rule of thumb is not to put personal information online as you will be hounded by some ruthless individuals.

A contact form where visitors can contact you is important. Research has established that if you have a contact form and your business details are on your website you are perceived to be a professional business entity.

6. Which e-commerce payment structure works best for me?

Two e-commerce payment systems are PayPal and Worldpay. PayPal has over 230 million accounts worldwide. Signup is free and very easy. During signup you can link your bank account or credit card to your PayPal account and uses the latest anti-fraud technology. You can easily add the standard Buy Now, Subscription and Donation buttons, or your custom made buttons, to your website. You can accept credit or debit cards and best of all you do not need a merchant account.

7. Who will I use for a web hosting provider?

Web hosting is leasing space where your website pages and files reside so that they are accessible to people on the Internet. There are a number of web host providers. Internet marketers use and recommend Hostgator. They host millions of domain names, have excellent 24/7 customer service and are very affordable at just under $10 per month.

With careful planning and strategizing you will get your business online and achieve growth.

Chapter 13

UPDATING YOUR WEBSITE WITH A CMS

CMS stands for content management system or another way to look at it is a system that manages website content. When talking about content management systems there is one system that stands out above all others and that is WordPress. What are the top three reasons to use WordPress as your Content Management System.

Number 1 - Ease of Use

You don't need to know html or web programming at all. If you can read, write and send emails then you can update the content on your CMS website. You just login to your websites administration area, write an article or page, put your keywords and other search engine

optimization data in and with one click of the publish button you've just put your content live on to your website and therefore to the world.

You can add as many articles as you want and queue them to publish on a certain day and time. Great if you are going on vacation. Write 20 articles and set them to publish every 3-4 days. That's nearly 3 month's of article writing you don't have to do and gives you time to do the jobs that need your attention.

You can easily edit any of your existing pages. Find the page your want to edit and make your changes. These changes could be altering the text font size or making a specific keyword phrase bold or italics. Click the publish button and once again your content is instantly added to your website.

Perhaps you have changed your email address from one provider to another and want to change your contact form on your website. You can do this as well. Your videos and pictures can be inserted, along with links to your other websites or services as it doesn't matter what kind of website you have.

Number 2 - Visitors will come and customers will come back

Because you are always adding fresh content in the form of articles, visitors will subscribe to your RSS feeds and to your opt in form. Search engines will be able to find your content as well as the spider bots constantly crawl to find fresh content. And if that fresh content is relevant to the site you will climb the page rankings.

Your subscribers get even more fresh content in the form of an email from you. This is where you give hints and tips, or let them know what sales you have, and the latest software that is going to help them in their business. Help solve your subscribers' problems by providing them with solutions.

Number 3 - As your business grows your website grows too

As you grow your business you will find that you need to add more to your website. Most businesses start in one direction and as time progresses and expansion occurs, the direction may change as well. The types of changes could be re-branding your business. With your website as a content management system it is a simply a matter of deleting your old logo and uploading your new one.

With new growth in your business your website should be growing at the same time. Adding more services, products or features to your website does require a little effort you can customize your CMS to reflect that growth.

Chapter 14

MARKETING

Internet advertising can be achieved via many mediums. You could set up different banner ads, send newsletters to individuals who have opted-into your squeeze pages or subscribe to pay per click ads. But before you attempt using all of these possible modes of online advertisement, it is imperative that you take a look at the nature of these online ads.

Social Media Marketing

Social media sites such as Facebook, MySpace, Twitter and YouTube have all become increasingly popular in the race for online advertising dominance. Because you can expect these social media sites to be filled with individuals from different walks of life all with different passions, you can find hundreds and

maybe thousands of people who are interested in your products and services. And you even get to interact with your customers on a level that will promote brand recognition.

Ezines

You don't have to sell your visitors various products right away to make money out of them. You can capture their emails and stay connected to them. All you need is to make a squeeze page where your targeted visitors can opt-in to your free report or ezine that you can send to their email address. You will be feeding them with information twice to three times a month. If they find your ezine valuable, most probably they will take your word for it and purchase the products that you are recommending.

Your own Blog

Search engines love blogs. Why? They are not static like a conventional html website. Blog owners are constantly adding more and more fresh content which creates a lot of search engine juice. They are extremely easy to add content and images to. Connecting to all forms of social media like Facebook and Twitter is as easy as a click of a button.

Pay Per Click

Pay per click advertisements can be really effective in reaching out to your target market although this certainly doesn't happen overnight. Essentially what happens is that you pay for every time a person clicks on your ad and visits your site for 5 to 10 seconds. Why do I say that it's great in connecting you to your target market? Basically, your ads will appear on a page that is directly related to your ads. Say you sell power tools. Your ads will appear in a website that contains information related to power tools. However, if you feel as if the campaign isn't working you will be able to review all aspects of the strategy and to reassess which parts of it are working and which aren't.

WARNING: A word of caution with Pay Per Click advertisements. It can cost you a lot of money if you don't know what you are doing.

CONCLUSION

There are many individuals, small businesses and large corporations enjoying the benefits of have a website.

Small and large businesses can compete on a more level playing field. A professional website presents a small business with panache and the wow factor just as much as big business.

Now that you understand the major principles behind the need to have a website for your business you're ready to turn absolute strangers into eager customers who are happy to give you their money.

There is no time like now to give your visitors exactly what they need.

Bond Global Enterprises is here to do that for you. Visit my website and see how I can help you get your website and business online.

Here's to YOUR success with building your business online today.

Faye Bond
CEO, Bond Global Enterprises
Where passion, empowerment and business meet
www.bondglobalenterprises.com

HELP FOR YOU AND YOUR BUSINESS

Need a Website? Do you want to know how to find your expertise, find your target market and build your business online?

Would you like a 15% discount on any website or coaching package to start to build your very own business online?

To qualify for the discount send an email to my personal email address of faye@bondglobalenterprises.com with the answer to the two questions that are below.

What is the #1 reason for using Wordpress for your website?

What Chapter did you find the answer?

(Clue: Can be unlucky for some...)

www.ingramcontent.com/pod-product-compliance
Lightning Source LLC
Chambersburg PA
CBHW041425050326
40689CB00002B/667